BUGS

BUTTERFLIES

by Emma Huddleston

Consultant: Beth Gambro
Reading Specialist, Yorkville, Illinois

Minneapolis, Minnesota

Teaching Tips

Before Reading

- Look at the cover of the book. Discuss the picture and the title.
- Ask readers to brainstorm a list of what they already know about butterflies. What can they expect to see in the book?
- Go on a picture walk, looking through the pictures to discuss vocabulary and make predictions about the text.

During Reading

- Read for purpose. As they are reading, encourage readers to think about the butterfly's life and the impacts the bug has on other things.
- If readers encounter an unknown word, ask them to look at the sounds in the word. Then, ask them to look at the rest of the page. Are there any clues to help them understand?

After Reading

- Encourage readers to pick a buddy and reread the book together.
- Ask readers to name three things from the book that butterflies do. Go back and find the pages that tell about these things.
- Ask readers to write or draw something that they learned about butterflies.

Credits:
Cover and title page, © Ogphoto/iStock; 3, © Axel Minguer/Shutterstock; 5, © leisuretime70/iStock; 6, © MR.PRAWET THADTHIAM/Shutterstock; 7, © K Hanley CHDPhoto/Shutterstock; 8–9, © Design Pics Inc/Alamy; 10–11, © Rudmer Zwerver/Shutterstock; 12, © mustafa_yildiz/iStock; 14–15, © Dmitry Potashkin /Alamy; 17, © Darkdiamond67/Shutterstock; 18, © PjrNature/Alamy; 20–21, © Ondrej Prosicky/iStock; 22, © Janny2/iStock, © Zoom Photo Graphic Stock/Shutterstock, © hwongcc/Shutterstock, © Miroslav Hlavko/Shutterstock, © Barb Elkin/Shutterstock; 23TL, © JodiJacobson/iStock; 23TM, © By Dalibor Valek/Shutterstock; 23TR, © koromelena/iStock; 23BL, © Nature Clickz/Shutterstock; 23BM, © tracielouise/iStock; 23BR, © Kerrie W/Shutterstock.

Library of Congress Cataloging-in-Publication Data

Names: Huddleston, Emma, author.
Title: Butterflies / Emma Huddleston.
Description: Bearcub books. | Minneapolis, Minnesota : Bearport Publishing
  Company, [2022] | Series: Bugs | Includes bibliographical references and
  index.
Identifiers: LCCN 2021026692 (print) | LCCN 2021026693 (ebook) | ISBN
  9781636913742 (library binding) | ISBN 9781636913810 (paperback) | ISBN
  9781636913889 (ebook)
Subjects: LCSH: Butterflies--Juvenile literature.
Classification: LCC QL544.2 .H835 2022 (print) | LCC QL544.2 (ebook) |
  DDC 595.78/9--dc23
LC record available at https://lccn.loc.gov/2021026692
LC ebook record available at https://lccn.loc.gov/2021026693

Copyright © 2022 Bearport Publishing Company. All rights reserved. No part of this publication may be reproduced in whole or in part, stored in any retrieval system, or transmitted in any form or by any means, electronic, mechanical, photocopying, recording, or otherwise, without written permission from the publisher.

For more information, write to Bearport Publishing, 5357 Penn Avenue South, Minneapolis, MN 55419. Printed in the United States of America.

Contents

A Beautiful Butterfly 4

A Butterfly's Life 22

Glossary 23

Index 24

Read More 24

Learn More Online 24

About the Author 24

A Beautiful Butterfly

A **bright** bug flies in the sky.

It lands on a flower and flaps its wings.

What a pretty butterfly!

There are many kinds of butterflies.

They all start as eggs.

Then, they turn into caterpillars.

Caterpillars eat and grow bigger.

Crunch!

Say caterpillar like KAT-ur-*pil*-ur

Soon, the caterpillar becomes a **pupa**.

It has a hard **shell**.

Inside the shell, the pupa changes.

Say pupa like PYOO-puh

A butterfly comes out of the shell.

It opens up its new wings.

Flap, flap!

The butterfly flies away to find food.

11

There are two **feelers** on the butterfly's head.

They help it smell food.

But the butterfly tastes with its feet!

Many butterflies drink sticky **nectar** from flowers.

They suck with long, tube-shaped mouths.

It is just like drinking with a straw.

Slurp!

The butterfly flies from flower to flower.

While it eats, it helps the flowers.

It moves flower **pollen** as it goes.

Flowers use the pollen to grow.

Butterflies need to watch out.

Some animals eat them.

Sometimes butterflies hide to stay safe.

Other times they fly away fast.

Most butterflies live for two weeks.

But some can live for a full year.

They make the world a little more beautiful.

A Butterfly's Life

Egg

Caterpillar

Pupa

Adult

22

Glossary

bright having a very strong color

feelers long, thin body parts that come out of a bug's head

nectar a sticky liquid from flowers

pollen yellow powder in flowers that plants use to make new plants

pupa a bug whose body is changing

shell a hard layer on the outside of an animal

Index

caterpillar 6–8, 22
egg 6, 22
feelers 12–13
flowers 4, 14, 16
food 10, 13
pupa 8–9, 22
wings 4, 10

Read More

Amstutz, Lisa J. *Fast Facts about Butterflies (Fast Facts about Bugs and Spiders).* North Mankato, MN: Pebble, 2021.

Sabelko, Rebecca. *Butterfly (Blastoff! Reader: Animal Life Cycles).* Minneapolis: Bellwether Media, 2021.

Learn More Online

1. Go to **www.factsurfer.com** or scan the QR code below.
2. Enter "**Butterfly Bug**" into the search box.
3. Click on the cover of this book to see a list of websites.

About the Author

Emma Huddleston lives in the Twin Cities with her husband. She enjoys writing children's books and spending time outside. She often sees the interesting bugs in this series!